About
Waterfowl

For the One who created waterfowl.

—*Genesis* 1:1

Ω

Published by
PEACHTREE PUBLISHING COMPANY INC.
1700 Chattahoochee Avenue
Atlanta, Georgia 30318-2112
PeachtreeBooks.com

Text © 2022 by Cathryn P. Sill
Illustrations © 2022 by John C. Sill

Edited by Vicky Holifield

Illustrations created in watercolor on archival quality 100% rag watercolor paper
Text and titles typeset in Novarese from Adobe Systems

Printed and bound in March 2022 by Leo Paper, Heshan, China
10 9 8 7 6 5 4 3 2 1
First Edition
ISBN 978-1-68263-234-5

Cataloging-in-Publication Data is available from the Library of Congress.

ABOUT
Waterfowl

A Guide for Children

Written by **Cathryn Sill**   Illustrated by **John Sill**

PEACHTREE

ATLANTA

Waterfowl are birds that live on or near water.

PLATE 1
Mallard

Waterfowl include ducks, geese, and swans.

PLATE 2
Canada Goose
Ring-necked Duck
Trumpeter Swan

Some waterfowl live on rivers, lakes, and ponds.

PLATE 3
Baikal Teal

Other waterfowl live on oceans.

Waterfowl have webbed feet that help them swim.

PLATE 5
Fulvous Whistling-Duck

Waterproof feathers keep waterfowl warm and dry.

PLATE 6
King Eider

Waterfowl use their bills to hunt for food.

Some waterfowl hunt for plants, insects, and small animals that live in shallow water.

Others hunt by diving in deep water for fish, crustaceans, and mollusks.

PLATE 9
Hooded Merganser

Some hunt for grasses and grains on land.

PLATE 10
Snow Goose

Many waterfowl migrate long distances as the seasons change.

They move to warmer areas to find food and good places to raise their young.

PLATE 12
Brant

Most waterfowl build their nests near water.

Some have their nests in holes in trees.

Baby waterfowl can move around soon after they hatch.

PLATE 15
Black-necked Swan

They are able to look for food and swim away from land predators.

Waterfowl have been useful to people for thousands of years.

It is important to protect waterfowl and the places where they live.

PLATE 18
Wood Duck

Afterword

PLATE 1
There are more than 170 species of waterfowl all over the world. They are found on every continent except Antarctica. Waterfowl live near water in all types of habitats. Mallards are able to live in most wetland habitats, including rivers, lakes, city ponds, marshes, swamps, and coastal areas. Most domestic ducks are descendants of Mallards. They are the most common duck in the Northern Hemisphere.

PLATE 2
There are three families of waterfowl. Ducks, geese, and swans make up the largest family. The other two are very small and include only three species in the screamer family and one species in the magpie goose family. Often ducks, geese, and swans form groups that feed together. Trumpeter Swans live in northwestern North America. Canada Geese live in most parts of North America. Ring-necked Ducks live in North America in summer and migrate to Central America in winter.

PLATE 3
Ducks and swans spend a lot of time on water. They have wide bodies that are flat on the bottom. Their legs are closer to the rear of their bodies, making it easy for them to swim. Baikal Teal live on marshes, lakes, and rivers in Siberia and in parts of eastern Russia and eastern Asia.

PLATE 4
Sea ducks are a group of ducks that spend the winter months on oceans. They only come to land to lay eggs and hatch chicks. Harlequin Ducks raise their young in fast-flowing streams. They spend the winter in rough, rocky coastal waters. Harlequin Ducks live in eastern Asia, northern parts of North America, and Iceland.

PLATE 5
Webbed feet of waterfowl act like paddles to push them in the water. These birds also use their feet to steer as they are flying. Waterfowl spread their feet to slow down as they land. Fulvous Whistling-Ducks live in freshwater marshes in tropical areas of Asia, Africa, and the Americas.

PLATE 6
Waterfowl have a dense outer layer of feathers called contour feathers. They also have special oil glands at the base of their tails. They waterproof their feathers by spreading the oil with their bills. Under the contour feathers are soft downy feathers that help protect them from the cold. Eiders and other waterfowl often line their nests with down to keep the eggs warm. King Eiders are large sea ducks that live along the Arctic coasts of North America, Europe, and Asia.

PLATE 7

Most waterfowl have a hook on the end of their bill called a "nail" that helps them gather food. The shape of the bill depends on the food the bird prefers. Some ducks that gather bits of food from the water have wide, flat bills. Waterfowl that eat tough plants and seeds have thick, sturdy bills. Ducks that catch fish have long, thin bills. Northern Shovelers use their bills to find food along muddy bottoms of ponds. They live in the Americas, Europe, Africa, and India.

PLATE 8

Waterfowl that feed in shallow water tip up their tails and put their heads underwater to hunt for food. This type of feeding is called "dabbling." Some dabblers skim the surface of the water with their bills, picking up bits of floating food. Northern Pintails are plentiful dabbling ducks that live in shallow wetlands and lakes across much of the Northern Hemisphere.

PLATE 9

Diving ducks live in deep lakes, rivers, and coastal areas. Their feet are farther back on their body to help them to move underwater. The location of their feet makes them move awkwardly on land. Geese and swans do not dive. Hooded Mergansers dive to catch insects, crayfish, and small fish. They live in freshwater habitats in North America.

PLATE 10

Geese and other waterfowl that feed on land can walk more easily than those that feed in water. Their legs are closer to the middle of their bodies. Webbed feet keep them from sinking into mud. Snow Geese have sturdy bills that help them tear off parts of tough plants and dig up roots. They live in North America.

PLATE 11

Waterfowl may fly thousands of miles each year during migration. Some fly day and night. Each year waterfowl migrate along the same routes called "flyways." Bar-headed Geese are strong flyers that can fly up to 1,000 miles (1,609 kilometers) a day. They can fly at very high altitudes and have been recorded migrating over Mount Everest. Bar-headed Geese live in central Asia.

PLATE 12

In winter, ice and snow may cover the places where waterfowl feed. They fly to warmer areas where they are able to find food. As the weather warms up in spring, waterfowl move back to where food is plentiful. Brants migrate farther north than any other geese. In summer, they nest in the high Arctic tundra, where the long days make it easier for their young to eat and grow strong. They spend the winter along the coasts of North America.

PLATE 13

Some waterfowl build nests on the ground near wetlands. Many hide their nests among plants. Others build floating nests from plants such as cattail and rushes. Ruddy Ducks sometimes cover their nests with plants to protect them from predators. Ruddy Ducks live in North and South America.

PLATE 14

Birds that nest in holes in trees are called "cavity nesters." Waterfowl often use holes made by other species such as woodpeckers. Nests in holes are protected from weather and predators. In some areas good places for nests are hard to find. People sometimes build nest boxes for cavity-nesting waterfowl. Common Mergansers are cavity nesters that live in many places in the Northern Hemisphere.

PLATE 15

Waterfowl babies are covered with downy feathers and their eyes are open when they hatch. Their parents do not bring food to the nest, so they must be able to feed themselves. Some baby waterfowl, including Black-necked Swans, climb on their parents' backs to hitch a ride. Black-necked Swans live in the southern part of South America.

PLATE 16

Land predators such as foxes, raccoons, skunks, and snakes often raid waterfowl nests. Swimming away from danger is the best defense for babies. Large fish, snapping turtles, and other predators that live in water are a threat to young waterfowl. Blue-winged Teal sometimes dive under the water to escape predators. They live in North and South America.

PLATE 17

Waterfowl have provided meat and eggs for people throughout history. Down feathers from eiders and other waterfowl are used to make warm bedding and clothing. Waterfowl living on farms eat harmful insects and weeds. People have raised domestic waterfowl for hundreds of years. Toulouse Geese first came from the Toulouse region of southwest France. They were brought to England and the United States in the 1800s.

PLATE 18

Waterfowl need clean, safe places to find food and raise young. Often the wetlands they depend on are destroyed when people drain and fill them. Fortunately, there are several international groups working to protect waterfowl by restoring wetlands and nearby areas. At one time Wood Duck populations were dangerously low because of habitat loss and uncontrolled hunting. Conservation efforts have helped to increase their numbers. Wood Ducks live in wooded lakes and marshes in North America.

GLOSSARY

continent—one of seven masses of land on the earth
descendant—an animal whose ancestors lived at an earlier time
domestic—not wild; tame
habitat—the place where animals and plants live
Northern Hemisphere—the northern half of the earth
predator—an animal that lives by hunting and eating other animals
prey—an animal that is hunted and eaten by a predator
species—a group of animals or plants that are alike in many ways

BIBLIOGRAPHY

BOOKS

ABCs OF WATERFOWL by Dave and Steve Shellhaas (Miami Valley Outdoor Media)
ZOOBOOKS DUCKS, GEESE & SWANS by John Bonnett Wexo (Wildlife Education Ltd)

WEBSITES

"Anseriformes," *www.allaboutbirds.org/guide/browse/taxonomy/Anatidae*
"All About Birds: Waterfowl," *www.kidzone.ws/animals/birds3.htm*
"Waterfowl," *www2.illinois.gov/dnr/outreach/kidsconservation/Pages/ArchiveNov2014.aspx*

RESOURCES ESPECIALLY HELPFUL IN DEVELOPING THIS BOOK

HANDBOOK OF THE BIRDS OF THE WORLD: VOL. 1 Edited by Josep del Hoyo, Andrew Elliott, and Jordi Sargatal (Lynx Edicions, Barcelona)

WATERFOWL: AN IDENTIFICATION GUIDE TO THE DUCKS, GEESE AND SWANS OF THE WORLD by Steve Madge and Hilary Burn (Houghton Mifflin Company)

ABOUT... SERIES

HC: 978-1-68263-031-0
PB: 978-1-68263-032-7

HC: 978-1-56145-038-1
PB: 978-1-56145-364-1

HC: 978-1-56145-688-8
PB: 978-1-56145-699-4

HC: 978-1-56145-301-6
PB: 978-1-56145-405-1

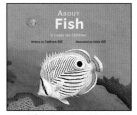

HC: 978-1-56145-987-2
PB: 978-1-56145-988-9

HC: 978-1-56145-588-1
PB: 978-1-56145-837-0

HC: 978-1-56145-881-3
PB: 978-1-56145-882-0

HC: 978-1-56145-757-1
PB: 978-1-56145-758-8

HC: 978-1-56145-906-3
PB: 978-1-68263-288-8

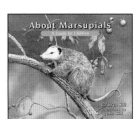

HC: 978-1-56145-358-0
PB: 978-1-56145-407-5

PB: 978-1-56145-406-8

HC: 978-1-56145-795-3
PB: 978-1-68263-158-4

HC: 978-1-56145-743-4
PB: 978-1-56145-741-0

HC: 978-1-56145-536-2
PB: 978-1-56145-811-0

About Reptiles

HC: 978-1-56145-907-0
PB: 978-1-56145-908-7

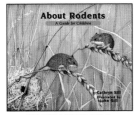

HC: 978-1-56145-454-9
PB: 978-1-56145-914-8

HC: 978-1-68263-092-1

HC: 978-1-68263-234-5

HC: 978-1-68263-004-4

ALSO AVAILABLE IN SPANISH AND ENGLISH/SPANISH EDITIONS

- About Amphibians / Sobre los anfibios PB: 978-1-68263-033-4 • Sobre los anfibios PB: 978-1-68263-230-7 • About Birds / Sobre los pájaros PB: 978-1-56145-783-0
- Sobre los pájaros PB: 978-1-68263-071-6 • About Fish / Sobre los peces PB: 978-1-56145-989-6 • Sobre los peces PB: 978-1-68263-154-6
- About Insects / Sobre los insectos PB: 978-1-56145-883-7 • Sobre los insectos PB: 978-1-68263-155-3 • About Mammals / Sobre los mamíferos PB: 978-1-56145-800-4
- Sobre los mamíferos PB: 978-1-68263-072-3 • About Reptiles / Sobre los reptiles PB: 978-1-56145-909-4 • Sobre los reptiles PB: 978-1-68263-231-4